PYTHON PALS

A PLAYFUL GUIDE FOR CHILDISH CODERS

Contents

4

1st Chapter: Welcome to Python

1.1 Why Python? Since it's magnificent!

1.1.1 Python's Charm

We should unwind the enchanted behind Python's prevalence. Discover the many reasons why Python is the language of choice, including its versatility and readability.

1.1.2 Python in real life

Investigate certifiable instances of Python in real life. From web improvement to man-made brainpower, perceive how Python utilizes its muscles across assorted areas.

1.2 Setting Up Your Python Jungle gym

1.2.1 Python Establishment Safari

Set out on the excursion of introducing Python on your machine. We'll explore through the establishment cycle bit by bit.

1.2.2 Picking Your Code Manager Experience

Choosing the right code manager is vital. Go along with us as we investigate different editors and track down the ideal one for your Pythonic ventures.

Get ready to enter the world of Python! The experience starts with the charm of Python and setting up your own special Python Jungle gym.

1.2.1 Printing Hi, World!

1.2.2 Fancier Prints: Organizing Enchantment

ChatGPT

Section 1.2: We should Play with Print

1.2.1 Printing Hi, World!

1.2.1.1 Welcome, Python!

Start your Python process with the ageless custom of printing "Hi, World!" to the control center. Watch as your first Python script works its magic.

1.2.1.2 Investigating the Print Realm

Jump further into the print capability. Learn to print multiple messages, variables, and even mathematical expressions using its various forms.

1.2.2 Fancier Prints: Organizing Wizardry

1.2.2.1 String Styling

Tidy up your printed messages with string organizing. Find the force of placeholders, f-strings, and the arrangement() technique.

1.2.2.2 Playing with Accuracy

Dive into the universe of arranged numbers. Control decimal places and investigate various styles of numerical data presentation.

Part 2: Meet the Python Zoo

Welcome to the Python Zoo, where Pythonic animals wander uninhibitedly, and every information type is a novel animal types ready to be found.

2.1 Presenting Factors: Python Pets

2.1.1 Embracing Your Most memorable Variable

Step into the universe of factors, your Pythonic pets. Figure out how to embrace them, give them names, and watch them store significant data.

2.1.2 Trying Different Types: Strings, Numbers, and that's only the tip of the iceberg

Find the variety in the Python Zoo. From string snakes to number elephants, investigate the different information types Python brings to the table.

2.2 Python Records: The Exhibit Creatures

2.2.1 Making a Zoo Rundown

Fabricate your own zoo with Python records. Assemble various creatures (components) and gain proficiency with the craft of rundown control.

2.2.2 Taking care of and Playing with Rundown Components

Get involved with your zoo. Feed and play with individual creatures (components) in your rundown. Uncover the mysteries of ordering and cutting.

2.3 The Strong Word reference Safari

2.3.1 Releasing the Force of Python Word references

Set out on a safari through the Python word reference wild. Catch key-esteem coordinates and comprehend the strength of this strong information structure.

2.3.2 Exploring the Word reference Wilderness

Explore the multifaceted ways of word references. Figure out how to look, alter, and remove data proficiently in this Pythonic wilderness.

Gear up for an intriguing experience as we plunge profound into the Python Zoo, getting to know the different occupants and their interesting attributes.

Part 2.1: Presenting Factors: Python Pets

Welcome to the Python Pet Reception Community! We'll explore Python variables, your new fuzzy, feathery, and sometimes numerical friends, in this chapter.

2.1.1 Embracing Your Most memorable Variable

2.1.1.1 Inviting Your New Python Buddy

Meet your most memorable Python variable! Gain proficiency with the fundamentals of variable reception, including naming shows and relegating values.

2.1.1.2 Taking Your Variable for a Walk

Take your Python variable for a walk around basic tasks. Witness how they respond to fundamental math and come out as comfortable with their way of behaving.

2.1.2 Trying Different Types: Strings, Numbers, and then some

2.1.2.1 String Songs

Plunge into the enchanting universe of strings. Figure out how to make, control, and link these text-based Python friends.

2.1.2.2 Mathematical Neighbors

Meet the mathematical side of the Python Zoo. Investigate the kinds of numeric factors, perform number juggling tasks, and hit the dance floor with Python's numerical ability.

2.1.2.3 Past Strings and Numbers

Find the adaptability of Python factors. Discover the significance of None, learn about boolean values, and experience the magic of dynamic typing.

Prepare to embrace your most memorable Python pet variable and investigate the dynamic variety inside the Python Zoo!

Section 2.2: Python Records:

Welcome to the Python Array Animals exhibit! In this part, we'll release the force of Python records - your cluster mates that blossom with variety.

2.2.1 Creating a Zoo List

2.2.1.1.1 Organizing Your Animal Troop Begin by creating your Python zoo list. Gain proficiency with the craft of gathering different creatures (components) and find the adaptability of rundown creation.

2.2.1.2 Settled Living spaces: Records inside Records

Investigate the idea of settled records. Make environments inside living spaces and witness the unique idea of Python's exhibit creatures.

2.2.2 Taking care of and Playing with Rundown Components

2.2.2.1 Taking care of Time: Controlling Records

Feed your cluster creatures by dominating rundown control. To keep your Python zoo lively and dynamic, modify, and add new elements.

2.2.2.2 Playing with File Toys

Hand out toys as files to your cluster creatures. Gain proficiency with the craft of ordering and cutting to connect with explicit components in your Python zoo.

2.2.2.3 Rundown Perception Safari

Leave on a safari through the universe of rundown

understandings. Witness the succinct and expressive way Python permits you to make records.

Join the experience as we plunge into the Python Cluster Creatures show, investigating the creation, taking care of, and playing with our exhibit partners!

Part 2.3: The Powerful Word reference Safari

Welcome to the Python Word reference Safari! Prepare to investigate the wild, untamed universe of Python word references - where key-esteem matches meander unreservedly.

2.3.1 Releasing the Force of Python Word references

2.3.1.1 Catching Animals: Making Word references

Become familiar with the craft of catching Pythonic animals with word references. Learn about key-value pairs and see how versatile this powerful data structure is.

2.3.1.2 Surrendering to Nature: Word reference Control

Release your command over word references. Investigate strategies to add, eliminate, and change key-esteem matches, transforming the wild word reference into a subdued friend.

2.3.2 Exploring the Word reference Wilderness

2.3.2.1 Investigating the Wilderness: Getting to Components

Explore through the thick word reference wilderness. Learn different ways of getting to components utilizing keys, opening the fortunes concealed inside.

2.3.2.2 Abilities to survive: Avoiding Mistakes To safely navigate the jungle, equip yourself with survival skills. Comprehend how to deal with key mistakes and guarantee a smooth excursion through your Python word reference.

2.3.2.3 High level Investigation: Word reference Cognizance's
Adventure into the profundities of cutting edge investigation with word reference cognizance's. Witness the compact and expressive way Python permits you to make word references.

Gear up for an exhilarating safari as we plunge into the Python Word reference Wilderness, finding the power and adaptability of this strong information structure!

Section 3: Welcome to the Control Flow Adventures

, Control Flow! In this part, we'll leave on an excursion through the Pythonic scene of direction and circling.

3.1 Conditionals: Dilemmas in Decision Making

3.1.1 If Statements: Simply deciding Explore the intersection of decision-production with Python's if articulations. Learn how to select actions and carry out particular code blocks in response to conditions.

3.1.2 Playing with Elif: A Fork in the Python Path Use elif statements to delve deeper into decision-making. Expand your Python code's adaptability to a wider range of situations by exploring multiple branches.

3.2 Circling into the Python Wild

3.2.1 For Circles: Navigating the Python Woods

Set out on an excursion through the Python Woods with for circles. Cross records, strings, and other iterable scenes, and figure out how to computerize dull undertakings.

3.2.2 Loops in a While Lost in the Python Desert

Explore the tremendous Python Desert utilizing while circles. Find out how to avoid getting lost in the loop by repeating actions until a particular condition is met.

Prepare for exciting experiences in charge stream, where choices and circles become your dependable sidekicks in the Pythonic wild!

Section 4: Capabilities Amusement park

Welcome to the Capabilities Amusement park, where Python capabilities become the dominant focal point and perform staggering accomplishments! Prepare for an exhibition of code wizardry and secluded wonders.

4.1.1 Defining Your Python Party

4.1.1.1 The Grand Entrance Enter the carnival grounds and develop your first Python function. Become familiar with the nuts and bolts of capability creation, characterizing boundaries, and executing your code scraps.

4.1.1.2 Capability Naming Event Investigate the specialty of naming capabilities. Create names that are memorable, expressive, and a part of the Python party's overall atmosphere.

4.1.2 Boundaries: Using function parameters to extend invitations to Pythonic guests is covered in 4.1.2.1, "Inviting Guests to the Python Party." Find out how adaptable passing values and constructing dynamic, interactive functions are.

4.1.2.2 The Boundary Jungle gym
Play with different boundary types and mixes. Make your Python party inclusive and dynamic by experimenting with default values, variable arguments, and keyword arguments.

4.2 The Arrival of the Capability Legends

4.2.1 Bring Proclamations back: Sending Python Party Attendees Home 4.2.1.1 The Farewell Gesture Use return statements to bid your Python party attendees goodbye. Comprehend how capabilities can send significant information back to the primary code, improving your programming experience.

4.2.2 Capability Decorators: Dressing Up Your Python Party 4.2.2.1 Creating a Python Pavilion Use decorators to decorate your Python events. Investigate this cutting-edge idea to upgrade usefulness, change conduct, and add a hint of polish to your code festival.

Part 5.1: Plunging into Article Arranged Python

5.1.1 Classes: Building Python Submarines

5.1.1.1 Blueprinting Submarines

Start your investigation by understanding the specialty of blueprinting Python submarines, otherwise called classes. Figure out how to structure and characterize classes for making objects.

5.1.1.2 Heading out with Characteristics and Techniques

Furnish your Python submarines with properties and techniques. Explore through the complexities of class parts and comprehend how they add to the general usefulness.

5.1.2 Items: Navigating the Pythonic Seas 5.1.2.1 Launching Python Submarines Create instances of classes to launch your Python submarines into the Pythonic Seas. Comprehend how to launch protests and release their true capacity.

5.1.2.2 Exploring Untamed Waters

Guide your Pythonic objects through the untamed waters of code. Investigate how articles communicate with one another and control their current circumstance inside the Pythonic oceans.

Section 5.2: Legacy Islands

5.2.1 Broadening Classes: Pythonic Genealogies

5.2.1.1 Sowing Seeds of Legacy

Develop Pythonic genealogical records by expanding classes. Figure out how to make kid classes that acquire properties and ways of behaving, shaping an organized order.

5.2.1.2 Developing Family Qualities
Witness the development of family qualities in your Pythonic genealogy. Comprehend how youngster classes can get to and develop the properties and techniques acquired from their predecessors.

5.2.2 Methods that Prevail: Undertakings in Pythonic Islands
5.2.2.1 Heading out to Pythonic Islands
Leave on experiences to Pythonic islands of code. Examine methods that are inherited from parent classes that can be overridden to meet the specific requirements of each Pythonic subclass.

5.2.2.2 Uncharted Territories

Explore Pythonic islands' uncharted territories. Uncover the adaptability and imagination presented by strategy superseding as you shape the way of behaving of your Pythonic subclasses.

Jump profound into the Pythonic Seas, investigating the standards of article arranged programming and exploring through the immense code waters with your Python submarines!

Part 6.1: Mixtures of Pandas

6.1.1 Preparing Information Edges: Pythonic Speculative chemistry

6.1.1.1 The Cauldron of Information Casings

Step into the enchanted universe of Pythonic speculative chemistry with Pandas. Gain proficiency with the specialty of blending information outlines, changing crude information into organized elixirs equipped for uncovering stowed away experiences.

6.1.1.2 Simmering the Pot: Making and Investigating

Find the privileged insights of blending the Pandas cauldron. Make information outlines, investigate their items, and figure out the mysterious properties that make Pandas a strong remedy.

6.1.2 Spells of Arranging and Sifting

6.1.2.1 Arranging Divination

Project spells of arranging with Pandas. Uncover the wizardry of organizing information outlines in different orders, disentangling examples and making your information get into the rhythm of your witchcraft.

6.1.2.2 Separating Charm

Investigate the specialty of separating charm with Pandas. Learn how to extract only the elements that meet your magical criteria from subsets of data frames.

Section 6.2: Array Magic: Numpy and the Art of Math-Fu Pythonic Kung Fu

6.2.1.1 The Craft of Cluster Enchantment

Enter the domain of Pythonic Kung Fu with Numpy. Become the best at exhibit control, changing your code into a power fit for taking care of mathematical information with artfulness.

6.2.1.2 Hand to hand fighting of Science

Investigate the hand to hand fighting of science with Numpy. Figure out how to perform strong procedure on clusters, making your code spry and dynamic notwithstanding complex estimations.

6.2.2 Direct Variable based math Divination

6.2.2.1 Projecting Direct Spells

Dig into the universe of straight variable based math magic with Numpy. Project spells of network activities and open the supernatural capability of controlling vectors and lattices.

6.2.2.2 Conjuring Changes

Summon changes with Numpy's straight variable based math magic. Figure out how to apply supernatural changes to your information, rising above the normal and entering the domain of the exceptional.

Drench yourself in the otherworldly universe of Pythonic speculative chemistry and math-fu, where Pandas and Numpy mix elixirs and cast spells that raise your code higher than ever.

Section 7.1: Pythonic Ventures

: 7.1.1 Embracing Your Imagination: Creating a Pythonic Castle Your Most memorable Task

7.1.1.1   Establishing   the Groundwork

Leave on the excursion of building your Pythonic palace. Establish the groundwork by characterizing the reason, degree, and elements of your most memorable undertaking.

7.1.1.2   Blueprinting   Pythonic Pinnacles

Diagram Pythonic towers inside your palace. Separate the undertaking into sensible parts, each adding to the magnificence of your Pythonic creation.

7.1.2   Overcoming   Pythonic Difficulties

7.1.2.1 Adapt to the Situations

Overcome Pythonic moves that push your abilities higher than ever. Tackle complex issues, carry out imaginative arrangements, and grandstand your authority of Python.

7.1.2.2 The Pythonic Win

Commend the Pythonic wins as you conquer difficulties. Enjoy the satisfaction of putting your Python knowledge to use in real-world situations and reflect on the lessons learned.

Section 7.2: The Python Experience Proceeds

7.2.1 Investigating Pythonic Domains: Past the Fundamentals

7.2.1.1 Graphing Neglected Regions

Set out on an investigation of Pythonic domains past the nuts and bolts. Jump into cutting edge points, libraries, and strategies that broaden the limits of your Python experience.

7.2.1.2 Dominating Pythonic Expressions

Ace Pythonic expressions as you dive further into the language. Investigate themes like decorators, setting supervisors, and offbeat programming to upgrade your Pythonic abilities.

7.2.2 Joining the Python People group: A Celebration 7.2.2.1 The Community Carnival

Participate in a gathering of the Python community to celebrate mutual understanding and support. Find discussions, occasions, and stages where Python fans assemble to share encounters, look for guidance, and commend everything Pythonic.

7.2.2.2 Your Pythonic Story Tell the community about your Pythonic journey. Commend your accomplishments, add to conversations, and motivate others as you become an essential piece of the energetic Pythonic people group.